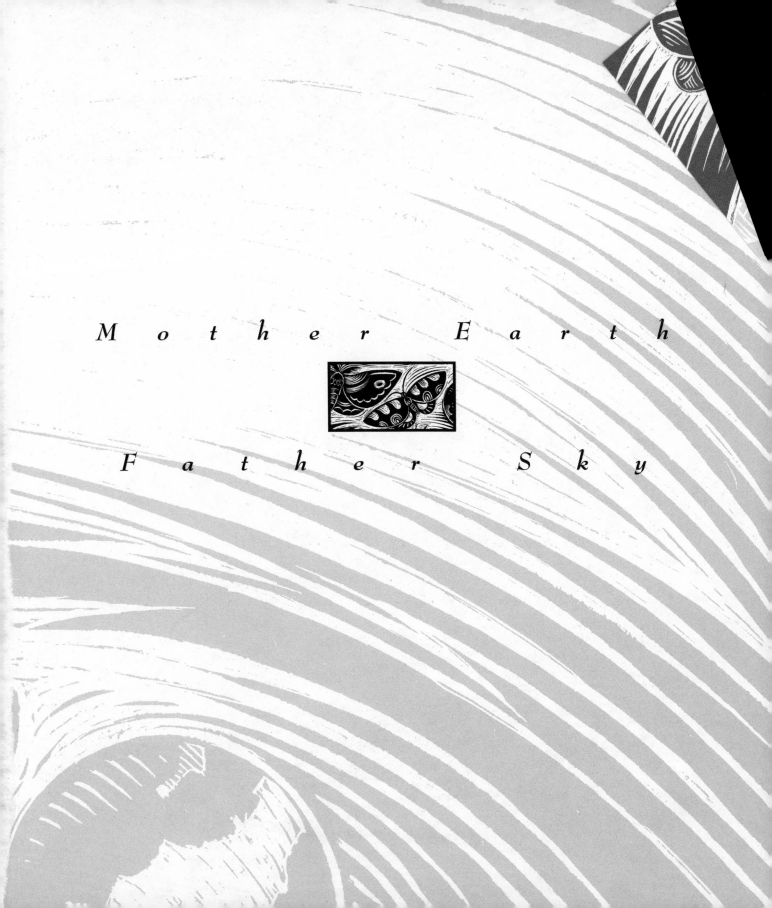

*M o t h e r   E a r t h*

*F a t h e r   S k y*

POEMS OF OUR PLANET

SELECTED BY

# Jane Yolen

ILLUSTRATIONS BY

# Jennifer Hewitson

WORDSONG • BOYDS MILLS PRESS

MOTHER EARTH

FATHER SKY

*Published by Wordsong*

*Boyds Mills Press, Inc.*

*A Highlights Company*

*815 Church Street*

*Honesdale, Pennsylvania 18431*

*Printed in Mexico*


*Publisher Cataloging-in-Publication Data*

*Mother earth, father sky : poems of our planet / selected by*

*Jane Yolen ; illustrations by Jennifer Hewitson.—1st ed.*

*[64]p. : ill. ;  cm.*

*Summary : An anthology of poems that describe the beauty and destruction of our natural world.*

*ISBN 1-56397-414-2*

*1. Earth—Juvenile Poetry. 2. Nature—Juvenile Poetry. 3. Children's Poetry—Collections. [1. Earth—Poetry. 2. Nature—Poetry.*

*3. Poetry—Collections.]*

*I. Yolen, Jane. II. Hewitson, Jennifer, ill. III. Title.*

*808.81/936—dc20    1996    AC*

*Library of Congress Catalog Card Number 95-60724*


*First edition, 1996*

*Book designed by Joy Chu*

*The text of this book is set in 15-point Bernhard Modern.*

*The illustrations are done in scratchboard.*

*Distributed by St. Martin's Press*


*10 9 8 7 6 5 4 3 2 1*

*Permission to reprint previously published material may be found on page 51.*

*For* MADDISON JANE *and her first steps on Mother Earth*

—J.Y.

*To my mom and dad,* DIANE *and* JOHN, *with love and thanks for giving me the earth and sky*

—J.H.

# CONTENTS

## CELEBRATE THE EARTH

SACRIFICE THE EARTH

S  A  V  E     T  H  E     E  A  R  T  H

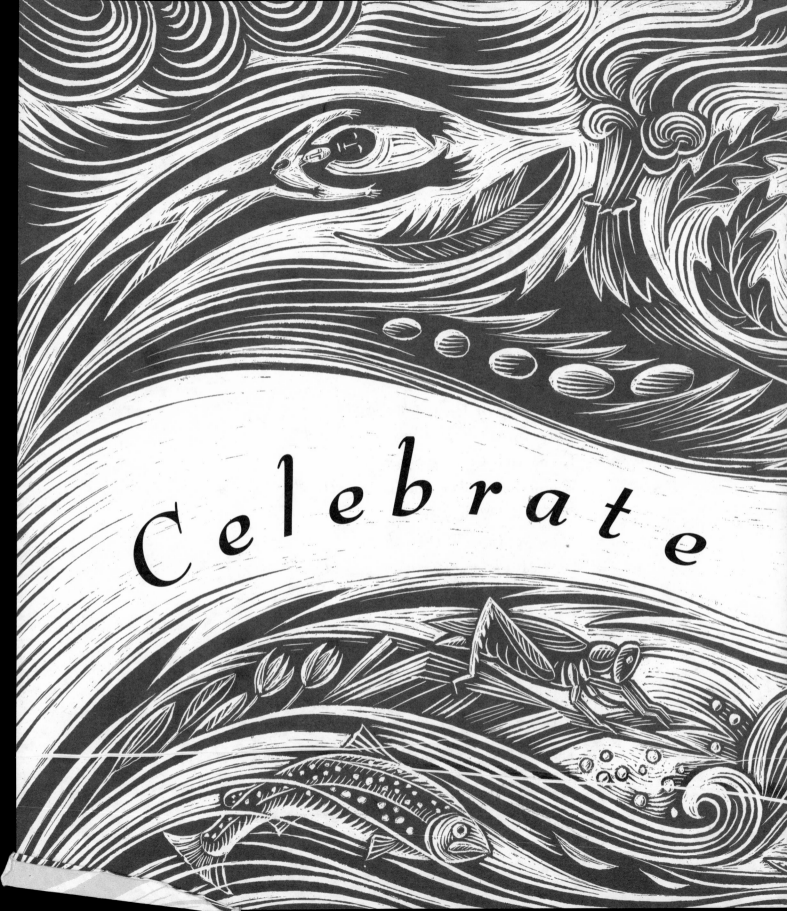

*From* TIMESWEEP

There is only one horse on the earth
and his name is All Horses.
There is only one bird in the air
and his name is All Wings.
There is only one fish in the sea
and his name is All Fins.
There is only one man in the world
and his name is All Men.
There is only one woman in the world
and her name is All Women.
There is only one child in the world
and the child's name is All Children.
    There is only one Maker in the world
    and His children cover the earth
    and they are named All God's Children.

*Carl Sandburg*

## TRYING IT ALL OUT

Earth
is a home of credibilities.
I dance
within her old gyrations like a snail.
How shall I ever leave this shell of stone?

Air
is an intricate bell.
All possibility
rises and shines in her transparencies:
that huge blue flower.
How shall I keep my tenement in space?

Fire
is the cooled stone of private desperations.
It burns
in all the old geologies of death.
How shall I ever warm this house of ash?

Water
is any bird flying, a wind, a wave.
Astonishment upon astonishment
washes our muscularities:
wings, jewels, and ponds.
Man is of water made; in earth and body
that is our buoyant home.

*Joseph Langland*

## WEEDS

What's down in the earth
comes forth in cold water,
in mist at night, in muttering
volcanoes that ring oceans
moving strangely at times.

And in autumn all the fields
witness forth: power there
where roots find it, rooms
delved silently and left
for the dark to have.

Up and down all highways
weed flags proclaim,
"Great is Earth our home!"
as we slip our hand
into winter's again.

Great is Earth our home.
Great is the sky.
And great are weeds in the fields.
We celebrate earth and air
as we sing in the wind.

*William Stafford*

## THE DELIGHT SONG OF TSOAI-TALEE

I am a feather in the bright sky.
I am the blue horse that runs in the plain.
I am the fish that rolls, shining, in the water.
I am the shadow that follows a child.
I am the evening light, the lustre of meadows.
I am an eagle playing with the wind.
I am a cluster of bright beads.
I am the farthest star.
I am the cold of the dawn.
I am the roaring of the rain.
I am the glitter on the crust of the snow.
I am the long track of the moon in a lake.
I am a flame of four colors.
I am a deer standing away in the dusk.
I am a field of sumac and the pomme blanche.
I am an angle of geese upon the winter sky.
I am the hunger of a young wolf.
I am the whole dream of these things.

You see, I am alive, I am alive.
I stand in good relation to the earth.
I stand in good relation to the gods.
I stand in good relation to all that is beautiful.
I stand in good relation to the daughter of Tsen-tainte.
You see, I am alive, I am alive.

*N. Scott Momaday*

## ON THE GRASSHOPPER AND CRICKET

The poetry of earth is never dead:
    When all the birds are faint with the hot sun,
    And hide in cooling trees, a voice will run
From hedge to hedge about the new-mown mead.
That is the grasshopper's—he takes the lead
    In summer luxury,—he has never done
    With his delights, for when tired out with fun,
He rests at ease beneath some pleasant weed.
The poetry of earth is ceasing never;
    On a long winter evening, when the frost
Has wrought a silence, from the stove there shrills
The Cricket's song, in warmth increasing ever,
    And seems to one in drowsiness half lost,
The Grasshopper's among some grassy hills.

*John Keats*

## AT THE DARK'S EDGE

Sister tree,
deaf and dumb and blind, and we
have ears to hear, have eyes for sight,
and yet our sister tree can find,
fumbling deaf and groping blind,
the field before her and the wood behind,
what we can't . . .
    light.

*Archibald MacLeish*
FROM "SEEING"

## THE BREATHING

An absolute
patience.
Trees stand
up to their knees in
fog. The fog
slowly flows
uphill.
   White
cobwebs, the grass
leaning where deer
have looked for apples.
The woods
from brook to where
the top of the hill looks
over the fog, send up
not one bird.
So absolute, it is
no other than
happiness itself, a breathing
too quiet to hear.

*Denise Levertov*

*PIED BEAUTY*

Glory be to God for dappled things—
　For skies of couple-color as a brinded cow;
　　For rose-moles all in stipple upon trout that swim;
Fresh-firecoal chestnut-falls; finches' wings;
　Landscape plotted and pieced—fold, fallow, and plough;
　And all trades, their gear and tackle and trim.
All things counter, original, spare, strange;
　Whatever is fickle, freckled (who knows how?)
　With swift, slow; sweet, sour; adazzle, dim;
He fathers-forth whose beauty is past change:
　　　　　Praise him.

*Gerard Manley Hopkins*

## BY FRAZIER CREEK FALLS

Standing up on lifted, folded rock
looking out and down—

The creek falls to a far valley.
hills beyond that
facing, half-forested, dry
—clear sky
strong wind in the
stiff glittering needle clusters
of the pine—their brown
round trunk bodies
straight, still;
rustling trembling limbs and twigs

listen.

This living flowing land
is all there is, forever

We *are* it
it sings through us—

We could live on this Earth
without clothes or tools!

*Gary Snyder*

## THE WORDS

Wind, bird, and tree,
Water, grass, and light:
In half of what I write
Roughly or smoothly
Year by impatient year
The same six words recur.

I have as many floors
As meadows or rivers,
As much still air as wind
And as many cats in mind
As nests in the branches
To put an end to these.

Instead, I take what is:
The light beats on the stones,
And wind over water shines
Like long grass through the trees,
As I set loose, like birds
In a landscape, the old words.

*David Wagoner*

## THIS WORLD

This world drives you out of your mind,
This night, those stars, this fragrance,
This tree bursting with flowers from top to toe.

*Orhan Veli Kanik*
(Translated from the Turkish by Talat Sait Halman)

## THE EARTH

When the earth doesn't shake, when the sky
is still, we feel something under the earth:
a shock of steadiness. When the storm is gone,
when the air passes, we feel our own
shudder—the terror of having such a great
friend, undeserved. Sometimes we wake
in the night: the millions better than we
who had to crawl away! We borrow their
breath, and the breath of the numberless
who never were born.

We know the motions of this great friend,
all resolved into one move, our stillness.
Why is no one on the hills where they
graze, the sun and the stars, no one
clamoring north, running as we would
run to belong to the earth? We come, we
celebrate with our breath, we join on the curve
of our street, never lost, the surge of the land
all around us that always is ours,
the beginning of the world and the end.

*William Stafford*

## I SING FOR THE ANIMALS

Out of the earth
I sing for them,
A Horse nation
I sing for them.
Out of the earth
I sing for them,
The animals
I sing for them.

*the Teton Sioux people,*
*North America*

Sacrifice

*the Earth*

## BUFFALO DUSK

The buffaloes are gone.
And those who saw the buffaloes are gone.
Those who saw the buffaloes by thousands and how they
  pawed the prairie sod into dust with their great hoofs,
  their great heads down pawing on in a great pageant
  of dusk,
Those who saw the buffaloes are gone.
And the buffaloes are gone.

*Carl Sandburg*

## GOD ATE THE BUFFALO

God ate the buffalo.
We are the mouths.

Hey, wolf. Hey, white-tipped weasel.
Hey, birds and haired things.
We are the mouths.
We are the mouths, mouths, mouths.
The Plains wolf lives in a corridor of wire.
He ate the meat,
but God ate the buffalo down.
And we are the belly of God.

Where is the Plains Wolf?
Now she whelps in the open,
in a mud run. In us. Of us. Eaten.
We are the teeth. God's teeth.
Teeth across the grasses.
Every blade.      Every
Thing.

*Mouths,          mouths.*
We are the mouths for the Plains.

*Barbara Ganzel*

## A CHILD IS SINGING

A child is singing
And nobody listening
But the child who is singing:

Bulldozers grab the earth and shower it.
The house is on fire.
Gardeners wet the earth and flower it.
The house is on fire,
The houses are on fire.
Fetch the fire engine, the fire engine's on fire.
We will have to hide in a hole.
We will burn slow like coal.
All the people are on fire.

And a child is singing
And nobody listening
But the child who is singing.


*Adrian Mitchell*

## THE BULLDOZER

Bulls by day
And dozes by night.

Would that the bulldozer
Dozed all the time

Would that the bulldozer
Would rust in peace.

His watchword
Let not a witch live

His battle cry
Better dead than red.

Give me the bullfinch
Give me the bulbul

Give me if you must
The bull himself

But not the bulldozer
No, not the bulldozer.

*Robert Francis*

## HARD QUESTIONS

Why not mark out the land
into neat rectangles
squares and clover leafs?

Put on them cubes of
varying sizes
according to use—
dwellings
     singles/multiples
complexes
     commercial/industrial.

Bale them together with
bands of roads.

What if a child shall cry
"I have never known spring!
I have never seen autumn!"

What if a man shall say
"I have never heard
silence fraught with living as
in swamp or forest!"
What if the eye shall never see
marsh bird and muskrats?

Does not the heart need
wildness?
Does not the thought need
something
to rest upon
not self-made by man,
a bosom
not his own?

*Margaret Tsuda*

## THE FUTURE OF FORESTRY

How will the legend of the age of trees
Feel, when the last tree falls in England?
When the concrete spreads and the town conquers
The country's heart; when contraceptive
Tarmac's laid where farm has faded,
Tramline flows where slept a hamlet,
And shop-fronts, blazing without a stop from
Dover to Wrath, have glazed us over?
Simplest tales will then bewilder
The questioning children, "What was a chestnut?
Say what it means to climb a Beanstalk.
Tell me, grandfather, what an elm is.
What was Autumn? They never taught us."
Then, told by teachers how once from mould

Came growing creatures of lower nature
Able to live and die, though neither
Beast nor man, and around them wreathing
Excellent clothing, breathing sunlight—
Half understanding, their ill-acquainted
Fancy will tint their wonder-paintings
—Trees as men walking, wood-romances
Of goblins stalking in silky green,
Of milk-sheen froth upon the lace of hawthorn's
Collar, pallor on the face of birchgirl.
So shall a homeless time, though dimly
Catch from afar (for soul is watchful)
A sight of tree-delighted Eden.

*C.S. Lewis*

## SONG OF THE OPEN ROAD

I think that I shall never see
A billboard lovely as a tree.
Perhaps, unless the billboards fall,
I'll never see a tree at all.

*Ogden Nash*

## THE FISH ARE ALL SICK

The fish are all sick, the great whales dead,
The villages stranded in stone on the coast,
Ornamental, like pearls on the fringe of a coat.
Sea men, who knew what the ocean did,
Turned their low houses away from the surf.
But new men who come to be rural and safe
Add big glass views and begonia beds.
Water keeps to itself.
White lip after lip
Curls to a close on the littered beach.
Something is sicker and blacker than fish.
And closing its grip, and closing its grip.

*Anne Stevenson*

# LIKE GHOSTS OF EAGLES

The Indians have mostly gone
but not before they named the rivers
the rivers flow on
and the names of the rivers flow with them
    Susquehanna     Shenandoah

The rivers are now polluted plundered
but not the names of the rivers
cool and inviolate as ever
pure as on the morning of creation
    Tennessee     Tombigbee

If the rivers themselves should ever perish
I think the names will somehow somewhere hover
like ghosts of eagles
those mighty whisperers
    Missouri     Mississippi.

*Robert Francis*

## REQUIEM FOR A RIVER

"So we diverted the river," he said,
showing blueprints
and maps
and geological surveys.
"It'll go in this canal now."

The Rio Blanco River starts in a glacier
up the white-capped Andes.
It has run through a green valley
for three million years,
maybe more.

Now in this year
when the Rio Blanco copper mine
at 12,000 feet altitude
gets underway,
the river has to go.

Pick it up,
Move it over—
Anything is possible.
Don't stand in the way
of progress,
And a 90-million-dollar mine.
"We concreted the dam," Bert said.

Thanks.

*Kim Williams*

## OKEECHOBEE

Cottonmouth white faces survey the marshes.
"Drain the swamps," they say, "we need
condominiums, jet-ports, room to spread."
Night is a reptile coiled in the willows.
Bulldozers whir in the dawn.

Herons and gallinules stalk the shadows
proclaiming: *invasion, invasion.*
Deer quiver like the water and are gone.
Huge bass deep in the cattails gorge
on their fry, and everywhere the strong
are holding their own. Survival requires control,
but lost somewhere in space the whooping crane's
final cry is speeding toward a star.

*John Allison*

## SEA CANARY

*The white whale, or beluga, was called the sea canary by eighteenth-century English whalers for its chirps and whistles and moans could be heard above the water.*

We heard her, white and weary,
singing a last song,
her whistle following us
into the night.
Did she sing of her young
still brown behind her?
Or of the bottoms of waves
made light by the moon?
Or did she sing her death,
the harps still heavy in her bones,
pulling her towards the air
and the long dark shanks of our hold.

*Jane Yolen*

## NURSERY RHYME

What do we use to wash our hair?
We use shampoo to wash our hair.
It's tested scientifically for damage to the eyes
by scientists who, in such matters, are acknowledged
to be wise.
Shampoo. Wash hair. Nice, clean habit.
Go to sleep now, darling.
It doesn't hurt the rabbit.

What makes lather in the bathtub?
Soap makes lather in the bathtub.
Rub-a-dub till bubbles bob along the rubber ducks race!
But don't get any in your mouth because soap has a
nasty taste.
Bath time. Slippy soap! Can't quite grab it!
Let's get dried now, darling.
It doesn't hurt the rabbit.

What makes us better when we're ill?
Medicine helps us when we're ill.
Years of research helped to develop every pill you take,
Like that one we gave you when you had a
tummy ache.
Cut knee. Antiseptic. Gently dab it.
Kiss you better, darling.
It doesn't hurt the rabbit.
It doesn't hurt
It doesn't hurt
It doesn't hurt the rabbit.

*Carol Ann Duffy*

## FOR A COMING EXTINCTION

Gray whale
Now that we are sending you to The End
That great god
Tell him
That we who follow you invented forgiveness
And forgive nothing

I write as though you could understand
And I could say it
One must always pretend something
Among the dying
When you have left the seas nodding on their stalks
Empty of you
Tell him that we were made
On another day

The bewilderment will diminish like an echo
Winding along your inner mountains
Unheard by us
And find its way out
Leaving behind it the future
Dead
And ours

When you will not see again
The whale calves trying the light
Consider what you will find in the black garden
And its court
The sea cows the Great Auks the gorillas
The irreplaceable hosts ranged countless
And fore-ordaining as stars
Our sacrifices

Join your word to theirs
Tell him
That it is we who are important

*W. S. Merwin*

## EXTINCTION DAY

The Dodo and the Barbary Lion,
The Cuban Yellow Bat,
The Atlas Bear, the Quagga and
The Christmas Island Rat,
The Thylacine, the Blue Buck
And the Hau Kuahiwi plant
Have all one thing in common now,
And that is that they aren't.

Give me one good reason why,
I wonder if you can?
The answer's in a single word—
The word is simply: Man.

Extinction Day, Extinction Day,
It isn't all that far away
For many animals and birds.
So let us decimate the herds,
Let's hunt their eggs and spoil their land,
Let's give Extinction a Big Hand,
For when it comes, it's here to stay . . .
Extinction Day! Extinction Day!

*Terry Jones*

Save

the Earth

### TO LOOK AT ANY THING

To look at any thing,
If you would know that thing,
You must look at it long:
To look at this green and say
"I have seen spring in these
Woods," will not do—you must
Be the thing you see:
You must be the dark snakes of
Stems and ferny plumes of leaves,
You must enter in
To the small silences between
The leaves,
You must take your time
And touch the very peace
They issue from.

*John Moffitt*

SCHOOL SYSTEM PRAYER

Teach my children evolution, telling time;
To name the birds, to know them—
The ones that sing now in the green place
Near the playground; to watch,
To give, to choose between
Damned near eternal pesticide
And season-hungry, crop-tail, fleckered
Starlings. Teach them music.
And naturally
Our story. Teach them
Numbers: pearly fathom, challenged
Acre. Bits of base two, base eleven.
Still, still—remind them of the Seven
Wonders of the Classic World—
The Light at Alexandria
Where Atlantis' refugees found haven,
Where Gypsies, having chanced the Gulf, tented.
Teach them Geography
Of old and new worlds, the words
Of tribes of Canaan and of Ethiopia,
Namibia, Zimbabwe and Azania;
Of the clans of the Short Well and the Deep Well;

The names of the Oceans of Rainbows and Tranquility
In the wet and dry quarters of the heavens.
Teach them how to change
Base metal into gold and not to always
Come in out of the rain.
Teach them to read
Signs
And while waiting in
—and between the—
Lines.

*Anna Kirwan-Vogel*

## THE SAMARA

Where are the samara?
Here. Here they are.

These rustling, whirling, words—
birds in flight from this page,
from this book.      Look!
From this soft, gentle breeze
they whisper,
"Plant trees. Plant trees."

Gaggles of winged seeds
circle and recircle,
sound and resound this advice
marking the sacrifice
this tree made for this book.
But look!
The words are birds in flight.
They whirl and twirl in circles
like winged seeds
and whisper gently in the breeze,
"Plant trees. Plant trees."

Hear? Here they are.

*Catherine Signorelli*

Wanting one good organic line,
I wrote a thousand sonnets.

Wanting a little peace,
I folded a thousand cranes.

Every discipline a new evasion;
every crane a dodge:

Bashō didn't know a thing about water
until he heard the frog.

*Sam Hamill*

## OH WORLD, I WISH

Oh World, I wish you were my mother,
For I would spread my fingers out
Against your earth face
And smell again the good brown smell.
I would feel your body warm by mine,
More than sun and fire and coals.
I would taste your silky streams
And the cold clean waters
Running over twenty-one stones.
I would lift my face to your sky.

Oh World, I wish you were my father,
For I would burrow into your marshes
And twine your green fingers in mine.
I would feel my face against yours,
Woody and barkish and rough.
And I would touch the slippery stones
As soft as tears and as shiny.
Your gray boulders, like muscles,
Would bunch up against my back.
I would lift my face to your sky.

Oh World, I wish you were my brothers,
I wish you were my sisters,
For we would play in the long grass
And the wind would swing it like hair:
*Swee-swash, swee-swash.*
We would make combs of acacia and thorn
And plait feathers in our braids.
I would share my bowl with you,
And you would share yours with me.
I would lift my face to your sky.

Oh World, I wish we were a family
Of flesh and earth and stone.
Oh World, I wish we were a family
Of blood and sand and bone.

*Jane Yolen*

## THE CAVE

Sometimes when the boy was troubled he would go
    To a little cave of stone above the brook
And build a fire just big enough to glow
    Upon the ledge outside, then sit and look.
Below him was the winding silver trail
    Of water from the upland pasture springs,
And meadows where he heard the calling quail;
    Before him was the sky, and passing wings.

The tang of willow twigs he lighted there,
    Fragrance of meadows breathing slow and deep,
The cave's own musky coolness on the air,
    The scent of sunlight . . . all were his to keep.
We had such places—cave or tree or hill . . .
    And we are lucky if we keep them still.

*Glenn W. Dresbach*